THE SIGNS OF
JESUS'
DEITY

IN THE GOSPEL OF JOHN-WORKBOOK

A BIBLICAL STUDY GUIDE OF THE MIRACLE SIGNS

SOLOMON E. FIELDS

ISBN 978-1-957943-90-9 (paperback)
ISBN 978-1-957943-91-6 (digital)

For more information, email: drsolomon@anchored4jesus.com

Printed in the United States of America

The design of this study guide is to supply the student with thought-provoking questions that will enhance their understanding of the material addressed in the publication, *The Signs of Jesus' Deity in the Gospel of John*. The ultimate purpose of John's writing, as recorded in 20:21, should point the reader towards faith in Jesus Christ, the Son of God.

Students who believe in the deity of Jesus Christ will be strengthened and encouraged by the application of these past miracles to our present-day lives. While the audience of Jesus' time struggled to grasp the signs as indicators of His deity, we can look at the Scriptures from a hindsight view and see the miraculous work of Christ.

The guide can be used as a tool for personal study, teaching in a group setting, and preaching the good news of Jesus Christ. The questions allow teachers and students to review the principles of the miracles and dwell deeper into how pre-suppositions, religious beliefs, and ultimately human choice could impact a person's faith in the deity of Christ.

The encouragement of my wife, Louise, and several pastors has prompted the writing of this study guide. My prayerful desire is for gospel preachers and teachers to apply doctrinal principles from the numerous concepts highlighted by the questions posed in the guide.

May the honor and glory of our Lord Jesus Christ be magnified.

STUDENT INFORMATION AND HELPFUL HINTS

1. There is no substitute for reading the Word of God. I recommend prayer and reading the chapter in John's Gospel before reading the book or study guide.

2. Plan sufficient time to pray, read and study. If possible, choose a time when you are not likely to be interrupted. The rewards of spiritual enrichment are well worth it.

3. Understand that the book and study guide is not an all-inclusive coverage of the miracles in John's Gospel. It is a concise tool to examine the miracles in John's Gospel that support the deity of Jesus Christ and enhance your faith.

4. There will be numerous theological and Christological applications that are relevant to our present-day audience. Teachers and students are encouraged to reflect on the uniqueness of Jesus's miracles and how they would respond to these in our current world. The book and study guide are useful as a launching pad for these discussions, especially in small groups.

5. Students should find the answers to general questions within the book's chapter and section. Some of the answers may cover multiple pages.

6. Pray and ask the Lord Jesus to provide opportunities to share your faith and knowledge of His miracles and signs performed. May the Lord bless and encourage your heart as you study this material.

STUDY GUIDE QUESTIONS

A. Chapter One - Introduction

1. What is the purpose of John's gospel? Discuss how John's gospel can strengthen your faith?

2. Discuss one theory of who is the intended audience for John's gospel.

3. Discuss whether the Bible can be God's infallible and inerrant written word and a reliable set of historical records.

B. Chapter Two – Literature Review

1. What was the primary language of the Israelites, and what was the language Jesus spoke?

2. Discuss the Pharisees' influence on the audience's mindset while witnessing Jesus' signs.

3. What was the purpose of signs in the Old Testament?

4. Discuss the meaning of "antilanguage" in an "antisociety." Identify antilanguage used today and the impact on communications across generations.

5. Discuss whether the misunderstanding of signs was a viable excuse for the rejection of Jesus Christ.

6. Discuss whether the lack of miracles during the ministry period of Jesus (Harvey and Jewish writings) could have been a factor in whether the audience recognized Jesus' signs.

7. Considering the Jewish doctrine of monotheism (one God), how did this viewpoint impact the rejection of the deity of Jesus?

8. Did Jesus' behavior as a sage contribute to the misunderstanding of the signs?

9. Give an example of Jesus using ambiguity. Discuss how these occurrences of ambiguity contributed to misunderstandings. Discuss how scriptural ambiguity can prompt the various religious beliefs.

10. What makes Jesus' miracles authentic?

11. Identify the two sign narratives in John's gospel that are in the Synoptic gospels.

C. Chapter Three – Jesus Turns Water to Wine

1. Identify several components of the first-century Jewish marriages that differ from our current marriages.

2. What is the perceived role of Jesus' mother at the wedding in Cana of Galilee?

3. Identify several characters mentioned in the narrative whose role appears to be for verification of the miracle?

4. Discuss the symbolism of the bridegroom in the narrative and our Lord Jesus.

5. Discuss the spiritual implication of inviting Jesus to a wedding.

6. Explain why Mary, the mother of Jesus, should not be elevated to a high religious status due to her request to Jesus, "They have no wine."

7. What was the purpose of the six waterpots of stone?

8. What can we learn from the servants' obedience to Jesus' instructions to fill the waterpots?

9. What symbolism can we draw from the filling of the waterpots?

10. How does turning water into wine point us to the deity of Jesus?

11. Based upon wine practices in the New Testament, should we believe Jesus made an intoxicating drink from the water in the pots?

12. Discuss the reaction of several characters who were knowledgeable of the miracle.

13. What does this miracle mean to you? Specifically regarding life's daily problems and crises.

14. Does this miracle of turning water into wine provide sufficient reason to believe Jesus is the Son of God?

D. Chapter Four – Jesus Heals the Nobleman's Son

1. What is the importance of knowing the location of Capernaum versus Cana of Galilee?

2. Does the writer of the Gospel of John imply that there are other miracles not recorded in this book?

3. Describe the faith of the nobleman and how people today are drawn to Jesus by crisis faith.

4. Discuss potential reasons Jesus rebuked the nobleman and the audience in John 4:48.

5. Discuss the simplicity of the spoken word of Jesus, "Go your way; your son lives."

6. How do we know the nobleman believed the words from Jesus? What can we learn from the nobleman's faith?

7. Name several factors that make the healing of the nobleman's son unique in comparison to other healing narratives.

8. What is the role of the nobleman's servants in this healing narrative?

9. John is silent about the faith and witness of the nobleman's son. What can we learn from the absence of information about the son?

10. Discuss whether you agree with Riggans' theory of the Gospels being the primary documents to gauge the audience's reaction to the miracles.

11. Discuss the mixed emotions of those who witness miracles of Jesus.

12. Describe the steps of faith for the nobleman.

13. Describe one factor in this healing narrative that makes it unique to Jesus as the Son of God.

E. Chapter Five – Jesus Heals the Man at the Pool of Bethesda

1. What three annual feasts were mandatory for Jewish males to attend?

2. What symbolism can we draw from Jesus being at the Sheep Gate?

3. Discuss the various theories on why sick people came to the pool of Bethesda.

4. Discuss the progressive way Jesus confronts the man at the pool of Bethesda.

5. What does the length of illness tell us about the man's condition?

6. What do we learn about Jesus' sovereignty and omniscience?

7. What is the psychological impact of Jesus' question, "Do you want to be made well?"

8. How does the response of the man show that he has misplaced faith? Discuss how we place our faith in objects as opposed to Jesus?

9. Discuss the power of Jesus' spoken word that supersedes human assistance or the water in the pool.

10. Can we conclude that the healing of this man produced little faith but not saving faith? Defend your answer.

11. What does this healing narrative tell us about the prerequisite of faith before healing?

12. Discuss whether this narrative focuses on healing the sick man or revealing the deity of Jesus Christ. What should this tell us about miracle healing today?

13. If the pool of Bethesda was previously a pagan healing center, what does this tell us about the boldness and power of Jesus?

14. How does Jesus justify His actions of healing on the Sabbath Day?

15. Discuss reasons why this healing narrative provides proof of the deity of Jesus Christ.

F. Chapter Six – Jesus Feeds the Five Thousand

1. Why did the large crowd (5,000) follow Jesus?

2. What annual feast did this miracle sign occur nearby, and is there a theological implication?

3. Why should we describe the multitude as potential disciples?

4. Speculate the reason for the test question of Jesus to Philip, "Where shall we buy bread, that these may eat?" How and why does the Lord test us today?

5. How would you describe Andrew, the disciple of Jesus?

6. How would you describe the role of Jesus, host, or guest at the banquet? Defend your answer.

7. What can we surmise about the limitation of humanity to solve problems whereby there is a shortage of raw materials?

8. What lesson do we learn from Jesus giving thanks before the meal?

9. What can people with food shortages grasp from this feeding narrative?

10. What can we learn about being wasteful with food (leftovers)?

11. Explain the difference between Jesus' feeding the multitude and Moses in the wilderness with the people being fed manna.

12. Give at least two reasons why the Elisha feeding differs from Jesus feeding the multitude.

13. What impact did the feeding miracle have on the multitude?

14. What can we learn about popularity from the response of Jesus to the multitude's intentions?

15. Explain Samuel Kobia's theory of the feeding narrative and whether it should be rejected or accepted?

16. Give reasons whether this feeding narrative is John's way of inserting the Lord's Supper in the gospel.

17. What should be the impact of this feeding narrative on the present-day church?

18. Discuss reasons why this feeding narrative gives proof of the deity of Jesus Christ.

G. Chapter Seven – Jesus Walks on Water

1. What was the natural environment of the Sea of Galilee, and why is this important to know?

2. Explain a potential reason that John informs us of the distance of the disciples' boat from the shore.

3. What theological implication can we gain from Jesus' response to the disciples' fear?

4. Is there an implication of another miracle in this narrative?

5. What is the possible reason (s) for John including this miracle in the gospel?

6. What is the impact of this miracle on the disciples in the boat?

7. Explain whether you agree or disagree with Elowsky's comments on applying this miracle to the present-day church.

8. Do you agree with Brown's opinion of the disciples receiving Jesus into the boat as an analogy of believers receiving Jesus in their hearts?

9. Do you believe this miracle sign gives sufficient reason to believe in the deity of Jesus Christ?

H. Chapter Eight – Jesus Heals the Man Born Blind

1. Where did Jesus encounter the man born blind?

2. What can we learn from Jesus's initial contact with the man born blind?

3. What Jewish belief prompted the question from the disciples, "Rabbi, who sinned, this man or his parents, that he was born blind?"

4. What role do the neighbors play in the healing narrative?

5. What is the primary focus of the Pharisees in this narrative?

6. Explain the symbolism of blindness and a sinful state.

7. Explain the steps Jesus performed to heal the man born blind and how these are unique to other healing narratives in the Synoptic gospels.

8. Name several interesting factors about the pool of Siloam.

9. Explain why Barrett's examples of sight restoration do not compare to Jesus' healing of the man born blind.

10. Why is the healing of the man born blind unique compared to the healing of blindness in the Synoptic gospels?

11. Explain the reaction of the parents of the man born blind when questioned by the Pharisees. Did the healing of their son prompt belief in Jesus Christ?

12. Explain why Jesus' healing the man born blind was considered a Sabbath Day violation.

13. What is the Christological issue in this narrative?

14. Discuss the progression of faith of the man born blind.

15. Describe the rift perpetuated between Judaism and Christianity due to the healing of the man born blind.

16. What is the impact of this healing miracle on the early church from a Christological perspective?

17. Give at least two reasons this healing narrative warrants belief in the deity of Jesus Christ.

I. Chapter Nine – Jesus Raises Lazarus from the Grave

1. What is a possible explanation for John distinguishing the location of Bethany?

2. How does the narrative of the raising of Lazarus highlight the motif of "life?"

3. How does John distinguish this Lazarus from the Lazarus in Luke's gospel?

4. How does John distinguish this Mary from Mary, the mother of Jesus, or other women named Mary?

5. Who does John use the term "Jews" to describe or identify?

6. Why does Jesus stay two more days in Bethany, beyond the Jordan?

7. Explain Jesus' statement regarding walking in the day.

8. Discuss the concept of Christian sleep as a metaphor for death.

9. How does the reader know that the disciples do not understand the meaning of sleep or the power of Jesus to awaken from sleep?

10. What is your reaction when the Lord is not present during the illness of a relative or friend? Do you respond like Mary and Martha?

11. What did Jesus mean by "I am the resurrection and the life."

12. Explain John 11:35 based on verses 33-35.

13. Discuss the Jewish belief of the soul remaining near the corpus until decomposition.

14. What are potential reasons for Jesus' prayer at the tomb of Lazarus?

15. Discuss the deity in the statement, "Lazarus, come forth!" and "Loose him, and let him go."

16. How does the resurrection of Lazarus differ from those in the Old Testament and other gospel resurrections?

17. What was the reaction of the chief priest and Pharisees when hearing about the resurrection of Lazarus?

18. What did Jesus do after the resurrection of Lazarus and the Pharisees plotting to put Him to death? Why do you believe Jesus behaved in this manner?

19. Lazarus' silence after the resurrection does it help or hurt the objective of proving the deity of Jesus Christ?

20. Do you believe the resurrection of Lazarus was an authentic narrative? If so, why?

21. How has the resurrection of Lazarus shaped Christian viewpoints of Jesus' power?

22. Do you believe the resurrection of Lazarus provides proof of the deity of Jesus Christ?

J. Chapter Ten – Debatable Signs

1. What was the scene in the temple before Jesus cleansed it?

2. Do you believe Jesus used divine power to cleanse the temple?

3. Based upon John 2:13-17, what is your opinion of buying and selling in the present-day church?

4. Do you believe the cleansing of the temple was a sign of the deity of Jesus Christ?

5. Based on the glossary definition of a miracle, was the cleansing of the temple a miracle? Defend your answer.

6. Where is the scene for Jesus revealing Himself to the disciples in John 21?

7. Discuss John's motifs of "night" versus "day" or "light" versus "darkness."

8. What does this narrative teach us about obedience before the complete revelation of Jesus or divine truths?

9. Discuss John's details of the campsite. Is this a reminder of Peter's need for restoration from when he denied Christ?

10. What symbolism can we draw from Jesus' instructions, "Bring some of the fish which you have just caught?"

11. Discuss the meanings of the 153 fish.

12. What spiritual symbolism can we grasp from the "untorn nets?"

13. Do you believe the large catch of fish qualifies as a miracle sign of the deity of Jesus Christ?

K. Chapter Eleven – The Ultimate Sign – The Resurrection of Jesus Christ

1. What day of the week did Mary Magdalene witness the empty tomb?

2. Why would Mary Magdalene think that someone had stolen the body of Jesus?

3. Why is the empty tomb fundamental to the Christian faith?

4. Discuss why the rebuttal against the resurrection of Jesus, based on the wrong-tomb theory, is a weak argument.

5. Discuss why the hallucination theory against the resurrection of Jesus is a weak argument.

6. Discuss why the theory of someone having stolen Jesus's body is a weak argument.

7. Please explain the difference between Jesus's grave clothes in the empty tomb versus Lazarus's clothes at his resurrection.

8. What can we conclude about the faith of Peter and John after witnessing the empty tomb?

9. What is the implied message from the angels to Mary Magdalene, and does the message differ from Peter and John seeing the linen cloths and folded handkerchief?

10. Who was the first person to witness the resurrected Christ?

11. What causes Mary Magdalene to recognize Jesus?

12. Discuss the symbolism of a shepherd and His sheep.

13. Discuss your understanding of why Jesus said, "Do not cling to Me, for I have not yet ascended to My Father."

14. What does Jesus's statement mean, "I am ascending to My Father and your Father, and to My God and your God?"

15. Why were the disciples behind locked doors after Jesus rose from the grave?

16. Why did Jesus show the disciples His hands and His side?

17. How is Thomas's doubt of the resurrected Christ indicative of people today?

18. What is critical about the confession of Thomas, "My Lord and my God?"

19. Discuss the additional eyewitnesses of the resurrected Christ.

20. Discuss why the resurrection of Christ is the ultimate sign of the deity of Jesus.

L. Chapter Twelve – Final Conclusions

1. Do the miracle signs in the Gospel of John, individually and or collectively, prove the deity of Jesus Christ?

2. Is there sufficient evidence from these miracle signs to warrant faith in Jesus Christ?

Additional Notes